PATHFINDER EDITION

By Patricia McKissack and Elizabeth Sengel

CONTENTS

Family

By Patricia McKissack

Ties

What makes you who you are? Part of the answer may be hidden in your family's past. Learn how to be your own detective and find the clues to your family tree.

What do you see when you look in the mirror? Maybe you have your grandmother's eyes or your father's smile. We inherit our looks and much more. From one generation to the next, families hand down favorite foods, games, traditions, and stories.

In fact, your family's past is made up of many different stories. You may have heard them shared at a noisy kitchen table or whispered on a moonlit porch. Who were your mother's grandmothers? Where did they live, and what were they like? Unique stories like these make you and your family special.

History Detective

Your family's history may be a mystery to you, but don't worry. You can learn about it through **genealogy**, which is the study of the people who are related to you.

Genealogy can help you piece together your family history. It starts with the relatives you know, such as your parents and grandparents. Genealogy also can take you back in time. You can learn about relatives who lived and died long before you.

If genealogy is like a mystery, then a genealogist is the detective who finds clues to your family's past. Often the clues are hidden in public records, such as birth, marriage, and death certificates. Some records show when people immigrated, or came, to America. Some tell where people went to school or when they bought land. Newspapers, letters, and those kitchen-table stories all hold clues, too.

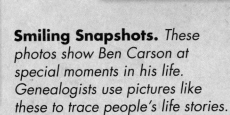

Smiling Snapshots. *These photos show Ben Carson at special moments in his life. Genealogists use pictures like these to trace people's life stories.*

Ancestor Names

Professor Henry Louis Gates, Jr., is a family history detective. He visited Ellis Island in New York, where more than 12 million immigrants first set foot in the United States in the 1800s and 1900s. Although Ellis Island is a great place to look for clues, Gates couldn't find records of his family there because he's African American. He knew that many African American families have an extra challenge when it comes to finding their ancestors.

The ancestors of most African Americans arrived in the United States aboard ships of enslaved people. They had no Ellis Island. Once here, owners bought, sold, and often separated members of a family. The owners gave enslaved people new names. Bit by bit, precious family histories were lost. Names were forgotten.

Professor Gates was determined to trace his roots and help other African Americans discover their family histories. In the PBS show "African American Lives," he explored the family histories of nine African Americans. One was the history of his friend Ben Carson, a famous neurosurgeon, or brain doctor, who pioneered many medical advances.

Beginnings

Ben Carson grew up poor in a tough neighborhood. His single mother, Sonya Copeland, worked three jobs. After school, aunts, uncles, and cousins provided a safe place for him while his mother worked.

At first, Carson didn't do well in school, but his mother refused to let him fail. She turned off the TV. She insisted he read books and write reports for her—even though she herself could not read. Once he started to work hard in school, things began to change for Carson.

He always thought he got his drive to succeed from his mother. But Carson knew very little about his ancestors. Were there records telling who they were?

Professor Gates began digging for clues, starting with old-fashioned detective work. He listened to family stories, searched for old photographs, and combed through musty records, including sales of enslaved people. He was even able to find a photograph of Carson's maternal grandfather.

Using public records, Gates also traced Carson's family to the plantation of wealthy white owners. They lived in Georgia in the 1800s. Their last name? Copeland, just like Carson's mother.

Amazing Breakthrough.
In this document from 1870, Professor Gates may have found Ben Carson's great-great-great grandfather!

True Grit

Then Gates found a stunning document. It showed how the white Copeland family divided up its property after William Copeland, Sr., died in 1859. That property included human beings. The record showed that a 2- or 3-year-old boy was sent away from his family and home. The boy's name was John H. Copeland. He was Carson's great-grandfather!

What happened to that child? Many separated families of enslaved people never saw each other again. Would this lead turn out to be a dead-end?

Amazingly, Gates found John's name again. This time it was in the 1870 **census**, an official count of everyone who lives in the U.S. John was about 12 or so, and enslavement had ended. Still, there was an even bigger surprise. John's name was listed with his mother's. Somehow, he had found his way back to his family.

"That was one hard-headed little boy," Gates says with admiration. Carson's reaction to his great-grandfather's determination? "Unbelievable!" he said. "Maybe that's where my mother got it from."

Back to Africa

The 1870 census held another surprise. It listed a 100-year-old man named James Ash who lived near India Ash, Carson's great-grandmother. James Ash's place of birth was listed as Africa.

Gates figured out that Ash could be Carson's great-great-great grandfather! Their search had led them directly to Africa. It's very rare to find written evidence of an ancestor who was born in Africa and sold into enslavement. For Carson, this is where the paper trail ended. But Gates had one more way to trace Carson's family: by using science.

In the Lab

Remember that look in the mirror? If you have your grandmother's eyes, it's thanks to DNA, which contains **genes**. These are our body's unique set of instructions, including how we look. Since genes are passed down through generations, a DNA test can point to the part of the world our ancestors came from.

Through DNA testing, Gates found that Carson's ancestors came from different parts of Africa, including Cameroon, Nigeria, and Kenya. Learning his family's stories "makes me feel connected," says Carson.

Your Turn!

"There's something wonderful about knowing where you came from," Carson says. Now a copy of his family tree hangs in his home.

You can learn about your past, too, just as Carson did. You might learn that your mother's mother ran a farm in Alabama, or maybe your great-grandfather worked on the Golden Gate Bridge. After you research your family history, you can make a family tree or a scrapbook.

Begin by asking the relatives you know questions—lots of questions! Who were your mother's grandmothers? Where did they live? As you talk with family members, take notes. Keep a section for each person. This will help you organize the information. Make sure you write down any names, dates, or places people mention. You also may want to record the conversations on video or audio tape.

Research

Once you've talked to your family members, you can start putting the pieces together. Draw a tree, like the one below. Write your name at the top and work down to your parents, grandparents, and great-grandparents.

Does your tree have blank boxes? That's all right! It's time for the detective work. Head to a library and search for family names in old newspapers. Visit City Hall to check out public records. You can also search the Internet. Keep a folder for family letters and photographs.

Remember, a detective is always on the lookout for clues. If you find an old family letter, look to see where and when it was mailed. Then you'll know where two relatives were at one point in time. Those places could lead to more clues. Bit by bit, you'll unlock your family's history.

Trace Your Roots.
A family tree shows how people are related. Each box represents a family member.

Mother

Grandmother   Grandfather

Great-Grandmother   Great-Grandfather   Great-Grandmother   Great-Grandfather

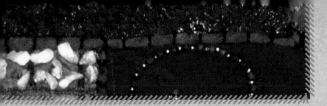

Share Stories

Family trees are just one way to learn about and celebrate your family's past. You can also make a scrapbook full of fun memories, photos, and other items.

Start by making a page for each of your relatives. Ask each person to write about a childhood story or a favorite memory. Decorate the book with family pictures, newspaper clippings, souvenirs, or drawings.

Keep adding to the scrapbook as you gather more photos and stories. At your next family event, pass the scrapbook around for everyone to enjoy. Invite relatives to add more personal tidbits. You might be amazed at the great conversations your scrapbook will spark!

Celebrate

Telling stories will keep your family history alive. Plan family reunions to trade tales. You can laugh about the time Great-Grandpa Max won the pie-eating contest or hear about the day Grandma Sylvia graduated from college.

Honor relatives who are no longer living by leaving an empty place at the table. Share a story about them before you begin the meal. You could also start a family newsletter to brag about your dog's latest tricks or your sister's piano recital. Take turns writing the newsletter so that everyone gets to help out.

Next time you look in the mirror, stop to think about the grandmother who "gave" you those eyes. Thanks to your terrific detective work, now you know a bit more about her!

Wordwise

census: an official count of every person living in a country

gene: part of a cell passed from parents to children that determines how they look

genealogy: the study of family history

u

Father

Grandmother

Grandfather

Great-Grandmother

Great-Grandfather

Great-Grandmother

Great-Grandfather

A Nation *of* Names

WHERE DID THE ANCESTORS of millions of Americans come from? This map shows how common last names are distributed in the United States. It gives a picture of the origins of many American families.

To make the map, geographers looked in phone directories to find the top surnames—or last names—in each state. Then they used software to identify which parts of the world the names came from.

The name Smith, which came from England, is the most common surname in the United States. What are the origins of other names? Can you find your name?

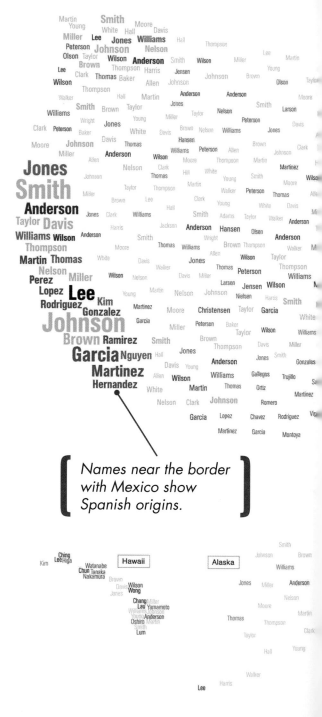

Names near the border with Mexico show Spanish origins.

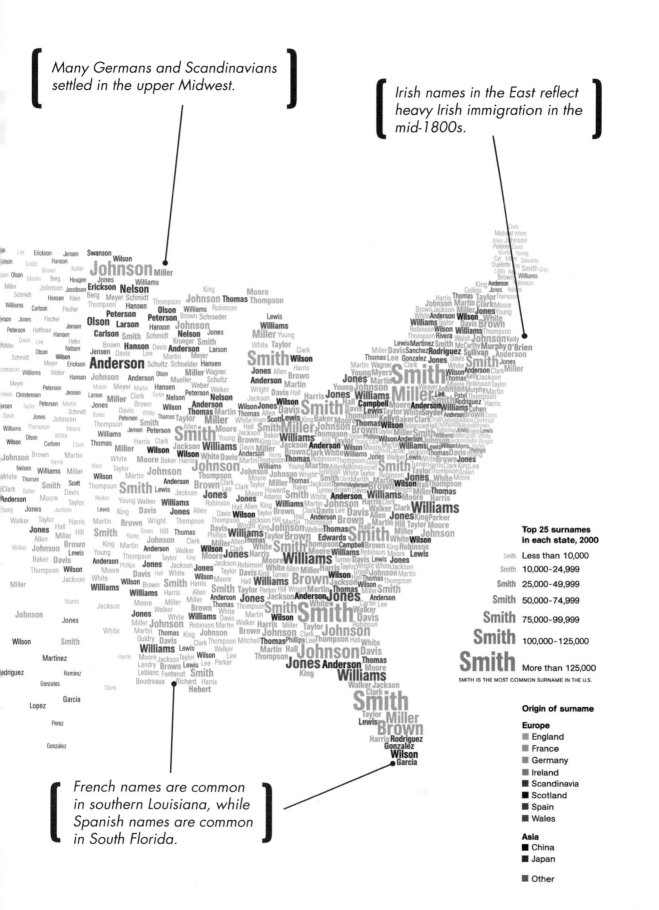

Many Germans and Scandinavians settled in the upper Midwest.

Irish names in the East reflect heavy Irish immigration in the mid-1800s.

French names are common in southern Louisiana, while Spanish names are common in South Florida.

**Top 25 surnames
in each state, 2000**

Smith Less than 10,000

Smith 10,000-24,999

Smith 25,000-49,999

Smith 50,000-74,999

Smith 75,000-99,999

Smith 100,000-125,000

Smith More than 125,000

SMITH IS THE MOST COMMON SURNAME IN THE U.S.

Origin of surname

Europe
- England
- France
- Germany
- Ireland
- Scandinavia
- Scotland
- Spain
- Wales

Asia
- China
- Japan

- Other

When people come to America, they bring more than their names. They bring a wealth of traditions, too. Here are four names from the map on pages 8–9 and some traditions that help enrich life in America.

Dragon Dance. *A dragon twists through the streets during a Chinese New Year parade in San Francisco.*

Summer Celebration. *Children from Lindsborg, Kansas, dance to celebrate the warm days of summer.*

Lee: CHINESE

Among many Chinese, New Year is the most important festival of the year. It is a time when family and friends get together to welcome the new year.

People sweep out the old year—literally! They clean their houses from top to bottom to whisk away the past. They put their money houses in order, too, clearing away old debts.

Chinese Americans celebrate New Year in January or February. One of the biggest events is a dragon parade. In China, the dragon is a symbol of strength and good luck.

During the parade, a long colorful dragon dances down city streets. Firecrackers whiz and pop. They are supposed to keep the dragon, who spends most of the year sleeping, awake during the celebration!

Anderson: SCANDINAVIAN

Everyone loves the long warm days of summer, but they are especially popular in countries like Sweden, Norway, and Denmark. In that part of the world, winter days are very short, so summer is truly welcome.

In fact, summer is so welcome in Scandinavia that people have traditionally celebrated it at a midsummer festival. It takes place in late June, when the days are at their longest and nights are short.

Scandinavian Americans carry on this custom. People dress in colorful folk costumes. Some women wear wreaths of fresh flowers in their hair. Dancers hold hands as they sing around the maypole, a tall pole decorated with flowers and leaves.

Traditions

By Elizabeth Sengel

Smith: AFRICAN AMERICAN

Many African Americans took a different name, such as Smith, when they came to America. They may not have kept their names, but they never let go of their skills and customs from home.

For example, the long history of textile work in Africa has led to the creation of many beautiful African American quilts in the United States. These quilts often have large shapes and strong colors, reflecting their African roots. In Africa, textiles were made with big designs and bright colors so that people could use the patterns of the cloth to recognize one another across great distances.

African American women create quilts for many reasons. They use them for warmth, to remember family members they have lost, and even to tell stories.

Memory Quilts. *This African American story quilt is in the Museum of Fine Arts in Boston, Massachusetts.*

Garcia: MEXICAN

The strum of guitars. The sweet strains of violins. The blare of trumpets. What is that sound? Mariachi!

The mariachi music that we know today got its start in the nineteenth century in the Mexican state of Jalisco. Today, it is popular around the United States. Mexican Americans—and many other fans—join bands to play mariachi music at festivals, concerts, and parades all around the country.

A mariachi band is made up of several musicians. They wear wide-brimmed hats called sombreros, fancy cowboy suits, and boots. The songs they sing are full of emotion. Many mariachi songs express feelings about love or nostalgia.

Mariachi Melodies. *Mariachi players draw music from their violins in San Antonio, Texas.*

Focus on
FAMILY

Answer these questions to celebrate the importance of family traditions.

1 How is a genealogist like a detective?

2 What steps did Professor Gates use to research Dr. Ben Carson's family history?

3 What events happened in the life of John Copeland, Ben Carson's great-grandfather? List them in order.

4 Choose one of the family traditions discussed in the article. How does it reflect family history?

5 Why is it important to celebrate family histories, names, and traditions?